MW00679094

My Marriage Is Broken,

Can It Be Fixed?

By Deborah H. Powe

My Marriage Is Broken, Can It Be Fixed?
by Deborah H. Powe

Published by Revealing Truth Ministries
5201 N. Armenia Ave.
Tampa, Florida 33603
www.revealingtruth.org

This book or parts thereof may not be reproduced in any form, stored in a retrieval system or transmitted in any form by any means—electronic, mechanical, photocopy, recording or otherwise—without prior written permission of the publisher, except as provided by United States of America copyright law.

Unless otherwise noted, all Scripture quotations are from the Holy Bible, King James Version. All rights reserved.

Cover design by Graphics Department of Revealing Truth Ministries

Copyright © 2005 Deborah H. Powe
All rights reserved

Library of Congress Cataloging-in-Publication Data:
International Standard Book Number: 0-9702097-2-X
Printed in the United States of America

Dedication

I would like to dedicate this book to Audrey Jones,
Linda Powe and my mother, Emma Hunt Stodghill.

Table of Contents

Forward

Over the past 21 years, I've share the events of the first 7 years of our marriage – the good, the bad and the ugly; mostly bad and ugly. I've shared my testimony of how God delivered me from alcoholism, adultery, unfaithfulness, poor money management, and just being a "bad husband". Yet, 28 years later we are still together, not just serving God together, but prospering in the will of God.

Now, you will hear the "rest of the story." You will learn how to live with an unsaved husband and still grow in the Lord. You will learn how wisdom from God will always bring you to a place of peace and prosperity, in spite of life's circumstances.

I believe Deborah's book will reveal, from her perspective, how God anointed her with wisdom and gave her the patience and strength to overcome. I thank God for my wife, Deborah, and for her enduring and not giving up on God and His ability to deliver.

I love her very much, and I realize what a jewel she is to me and to the Body of Christ.

—Gregory Powe

Part I: Lost and Found

Chapter One:
Great Expectations

A couple who start off their marriage when they are non-Christians have a tough row to hoe, but my husband, Greg, and I are living proof that God can turn even the hardest of marital situations around. When talking about the course of our marriage, we often say that we have been married three times. That seems to best sum up the fact that our marriage has had three very distinct stages: the stage when neither of us was born again, the stage when I was born again and he was not, and the stage when we were both born again.

During the first three years of our marriage neither Greg nor I was saved. Looking back, I do not think either of us thought during those early years that we would still be together twenty-eight years later, but God's grace has brought us far beyond our expectations. "Now unto him that is able to do exceeding abundantly above all that we ask or think, according to the power that worketh in us" (Eph. 3:20).

After I graduated from the University of South Alabama, I had very high hopes for the future when Greg and I married in the fall of 1976, in Mobile, Alabama. I was getting married to the love of my life and had a good job. Initially, we were going to have a courthouse ceremony in order to save money to rent and furnish our apartment. At the last minute, with a little coaching, we decided to have a small ceremony with close friends and relatives at our best friends', Linda and Wayne's apartment.

I had been sewing since high school so I decided to make my own dress. It was a simple high bodice, "A" line dress with a train

1

decorated with lace and sequins. The veil was made to match with the same decorative pattern as the dress. Linda purchased the cake which was decorated with plastic wedding rings. Because I wanted nicer rings than Greg and I could afford, we delayed the purchase of wedding rings and used the ones from the cake for the ceremony and pictures.

At the time, I thought Greg and I were being practical, had sound judgment and were pretty good people. We were not moved by what we thought were petty details, including our idea concerning church and God.

We both acknowledged our belief in God, but that is where our discussion of God ended prior to our wedding. We never once talked about attending church or our relationship with God. In my case, I could have been classified as one of the hardest persons for a Christian to witness to about the need for salvation because I thought I was already "good", and therefore, did not need to do anything more than go to church on Sundays. I was quite self-righteous. Oh, I did not do the bad stuff that "those heathens did", like drink and do drugs. No, not me; I was just fine…or so I thought.

Life was about to throw me such a curve ball, however, I would learn I needed God much more than I could have begun to realize at the time. I would find myself in such hardship that I would become desperate for His help. This would be after I tried to work it all out on my own, of course. But the time would come when I would discover that refraining from outright sin and going to church were not enough, and I would have to put all of my trust in God.

When I entered into marriage I had a form of godliness, but no knowledge of the power of God or the grace of God. In essence, I did what I thought I was supposed to do but had not been born again by the

Spirit of God.

> *For I bear them record that they have a zeal of God, but not according to knowledge. For they being ignorant of God's righteousness, and going about to establish their own righteousness, have not submitted themselves unto the righteousness of God.*
>
> —Romans 10:2-3

Even before we were married, my husband for one reason or another did not go to church at all. Maybe this was because he thought trying to mix his lifestyle with church attendance would be hypocritical. Or maybe it was because he simply had made the decision to not go. Either way, he was certainly not inclined, as I was, to go through the motions of doing what other people thought he was supposed to do. I should have seen this as a red flag, but I did not. I was judging by how I felt about him and how I thought he felt about me. I simply assumed that being in love meant that we should get married. So, in spite of our different views on going to church, we were married. Because both of us were lost, neither of us knew much about God, and neither of us had a personal relationship with Him. Of course, this spelled trouble for us, individually and as a couple.

Expectations Unfulfilled

These first seven years of my marriage were the most infuriating, frustrating, difficult and challenging times of my life. Like most people, I entered into matrimony with high expectations that were based on wrong information; I was wide open to much despair and disappointment.

3

Nothing about this union was even remotely based on the principles of God. I just knew I was in love and thought marriage should be the natural course to follow courtship—after all, most of my college friends were already married. Nothing had prepared me for the collision course I was on.

In order to conquer the challenges awaiting me, I needed a lot more than going through ritualistic motions of just attending church and "being good" according to my own standards. Not knowing of the power of God to deliver and having no idea that I needed to be delivered from anything, it took an invasion of the power of God to first change me and then change my situation. I needed to actually develop a real relationship with God, so I could see through His eyes rather than through the eyes of a disappointed bride.

Like most women, I had my own ideas of what I thought my life and my marriage should be like. I had always planned, and even assumed, that I would be successful in every aspect of my life. My expectation of personal success was the canvas on which I had painted the very detailed picture of what I expected my life to be like.

In this picture, I would be a successful college student, a happily married wife and a joyful mother raising children. My idea included lots of happy hours with my husband, spending time together enjoying each other and our children. My loving husband would surely be home for dinner every night, where we would talk and laugh and instruct our beautiful, well-behaved children. We had plenty of money, a lovely home in the suburbs with a white picket fence, and peace and order in every corner of our existence.

I fully expected my family to be just like the sitcom called "The Leave It To Beaver Show", that was very popular during the '60s. The

4

husband, wife and two children had breakfast together every morning before the children went off to school. The husband went off to a secure job where he was successful, and the mother remained at home to prepare for her family's return to an immaculate house with dinner on the table.

With all of these expectations and absolutely no preparation for real life, I was sorely disappointed when reality did not unfold according to the picture I had in my mind. It had never crossed my mind that Greg's picture of how marriage "ought to be" was very different from my own. I had assumed that Greg's ideals matched my own. We had not had the benefit of the pre-marital counseling principles that Greg and I now provide couples planning to be married. Because we had never talked about the ground rules of married life or the roles of a husband and wife; we did not even know what we expected from one another.

Greg and I had no awareness of the other's perspective; we sometimes made sweeping assumptions about one another's intentions. Crashes were inevitable because we were flying at cross-purposes with each other in separate planes, and life started to feel more like a collision course than the TV family sitcom where there was little or no turbulence. It took years to begin to understand that our disagreements were rooted in differing points of view.

Unspoken Roles and Expectations

Unfortunately, the lack of communication before marriage can pose some challenging situations. My mother knew this, so it stands to reason that the first question she asked me when I so cheerfully informed her that Greg had asked me to marry him was, "Can you two talk to each other?" Not understanding the question, I quickly answered, "Yes, we talk all the time." Then, rather than paying any attention to her response of "It is so important that you two are able to communicate with each other," I slipped into an imaginary state of mind, believing that all was well in "Deborah's world".

Little did I know that Greg's and my failure to communicate before our marriage was setting us up for much havoc. The differences in our opinions, expectations, goals and understanding of marital roles began to surface soon after we were married. Like so many others who go "brain-dead" and allow their emotions to direct them when they are making a decision, my mind had become deceived and my conscience was denied its normal standard of judgment.

Our differences ranged from eating to sleeping. Greg's home life while he was growing up had been a little more relaxed and casual than mine. In my home we ate breakfast and dinner together at the table. There, we had joyful conversations and received a little correction now and then. Because of this background, I was quite surprised when I prepared our first breakfast and discovered that Greg wanted to eat it in the bedroom in front of the television, instead of at the table. To top it off, he wanted rice with cheese, instead of what I would have called "normal" breakfast food.

For dinner, I would prepare a well-balanced meal consisting of two vegetables, one starch and a meat. When he would request two starches, I would say that having two would be "unhealthy" and would refuse to cook the second starch. We often had spats about my cooking, from how it tasted, to what I prepared. It got to the point that when he asked what was for dinner, I would not tell him because I did not want to hear the criticism. Greg responded by buying fast food on his way home. I was so upset when he started stopping for fast food and only purchased enough for himself after I had worked all day and cooked dinner. This was just one of the many kinds of collisions we had.

Our sleep habits were also different. Greg was a night person; staying up until 1 or 2 a.m. was normal for him. I, on the other hand, thought 10 p.m. was pushing it when you had to go to work the next morning. Sure, we had stayed out late sometimes while we were dating, but only if I did not have an early class the next morning. Little did I know that Greg's night had just begun when he would drop me off so I could get to bed early.

Our views on finances were also different. I believed you should pay your bills, and Greg believed you pay them when and if you wanted to. I wanted to buy a house, but he wanted to rent because he did not want the responsibility of cutting the grass. I wanted to save money; he wanted to spend it all right away. Greg did not believe in saving, and he certainly did not believe in tithing. I actually would get cash to pay my tithe so he would not see the cancelled checks and start an argument with me over it.

What really blew me away was that Greg did not seem to see the importance of keeping a steady job. Greg would find employment and would even advance on the job, but anytime a demand was placed on him that conflicted with what he wanted to do, he would quit. Greg told me once that he had to leave his job because they were requiring him to work one Sunday per month. His reasoning was "people go to church on Sunday." I said, "But you don't go to church." He just looked at me and said, "Well, I might want to go one day."

Greg went through so many jobs that I lost count. He once

worked as a private investigator where he used a number of aliases. At tax time we were getting so many W-2s under different names that I refused to file jointly with him. At one point, Greg was without employment for a span of about eight months. He picked me up from work one Friday during this time of unemployment and explained to me that he needed a vacation. I was furious with him. He left with the new car and did not return until three days later.

After having learned the hard way, I now counsel engaged couples to "investigate before you invest." It would have helped if I had just spent more time around his relatives, so I could hear what they had to say about Greg and see how they interacted with him. Really, listening to his friends' comments about past experiences would have helped. Also, allowing my friends to critique Greg would have given me more insight. Having him spend more time around my family so they could have more input would have provided me with informed counsel from people who loved me and wanted what was best for me.

For which of you, intending to build a tower, sitteth not down first, and counteth the cost, whether he have sufficient to finish it? Lest haply, after he hath laid the foundation, and is not able to finish it, all that behold it begin to mock him, Saying, This man began to build, and was not able to finish. Or what king, going to make war against another king, sitteth not down first, and consulteth whether he be able with ten thousand to meet him that cometh against him with twenty thousand?

—Luke 14:28-31

I found out later that most of Greg's family thought he was quite spoiled because he usually got everything he wanted and suffered very few consequences when he did something wrong. It seemed that he had always been able to talk himself out of any situation he got himself into. From age fourteen, Greg worked during the summers at the same company where his father was employed. He earned well above minimum wage and was allowed to spend his earnings as he pleased.

Contrary to this, I earned a small allowance of twenty dollars every two weeks, which I would spend on things my mother did not consider necessities; things like makeup, nail polish, stockings and junk food. I even had to share the junk food with my brothers and sisters. I was also expected to acquire my own funding for my college education. This involved keeping up with a full-time class load and two work-study jobs that enabled me to purchase my books and class supplies. If I had any money left over, I would buy the clothes I needed, most of the time paying for what I had put on layaway. I would purchase food with the twenty dollars my parents sent me each week. I really could stretch a dollar. These were the differing experiences and responsibilities that shaped the opposing financial expectations and values that Greg and I brought into our marriage.

Everybody puts their best foot forward when they are dating. That foot, however, is not the foot to be concerned with. Instead, those who are dating should be looking for the foot hiding under the table. In retrospect, I see that all the signs were present, but I ignored them. Greg was flamboyant, excessive, carefree and unafraid of unordinary experiences. Contrarily, I was very conservative, modest and down-to-earth. However, the dream of wanting to be married, the gradual pressure of seeing my friends get married, and not wanting to think I had wasted so much of my time with a man who wasn't going to marry me, were the major factors that played into my willful ignorance and poor judgment. I had not done the investigation necessary to count the cost and I had not been patient.

> *But let patience have her perfect work, that ye may be perfect and entire, wanting nothing.*
>
> —James 1:4

Marriage is a covenant instituted by God, and any time there is a covenant involved, there should be much conversation between all parties; the couple and the family members and friends that the couple's relationship will affect. Productive conversations about the division of labor, financial goals, raising children, personal goals, and our relatives' involvement in our lives would have done more for me than a thousand romantic dinners.

Greg and I were clueless when it came to the biblical blueprint for marriage. That is why we now are so adamant about potential marital couples participating in marriage counseling before setting a wedding date. We work to ensure that they examine the facts and not allow their judgment to be clouded by the excitement surrounding the idea of getting married. Greg often tells couples "concentrate on your marriage, not on the wedding, because the wedding is just one day and it is not even all day."

Chapter Two:
Disappointment Settles In

Greg's view of marriage and my dream of marriage were so far apart that within a few short months, our marriage felt like the covenant from hell. This was my view of the marriage at any rate. Greg, on the other hand, seemed perfectly content.

Stunned

When I entered into the marriage, I thought our love would conquer all. I thought it would conquer our differences. I never doubted that I would be happy and that our marriage would match that "Ward and June Cleaver" picture perfect image I had in my mind. When I said, "I do", I was sure he adored me. But within a month, I was wondering if he loved me at all.

I relentlessly tried to make Greg conform to my dream of marriage, but it was all to no avail. He outright refused to act like a married man with responsibilities. I once made the mistake of comparing our marriage to our best friends' marriage. That, of course, infuriated him because it was a powerful blow to his ego. I advise against ever doing this because it is sure to lead to even more problems.

As it turns out, my husband was very, very restless. He always had to be doing something, and because he was not born again, you can imagine what some of the things were he thought he had to do. Greg required very little sleep, four to five hours a night. Therefore, when everyone else was sleeping, he was wide-awake and looking for something to do. Back then there was no such thing as cable or satellite TV, so the last station signed off at 10:30 p.m. He looked elsewhere for his "something to do."

Often, he would come home from work, happily announcing the opening of the newest nightclub. Of course, he just had to go check it out. Going out on the weekends was not enough for Greg, only clubbing every night would do. Regardless of the amount of money he had, be it little or a lot, he always came back drunk. I could only assume that people were buying him drinks. As the saying goes, "the world takes care of its own."

Like most in my situation, I had gone into the marriage assuming that Greg would settle into married life and relinquish the single lifestyle of no accountability or responsibility to anyone. I was wrong as "two left shoes". To Greg, marriage was a means for him to get the financial help he needed to move out of his parents' house. Greg's suggestion that we live together should have been my clue that he really was not interested in the marriage covenant. Instead, I turned my eyes away from this as well, and became adamant about not living with any man before marriage. Rather than seeing his request as being a sign of things to come, I focused on what "shacking up" with a man would do to my "good girl" image. Looking back, I think he was being propelled by the notion that having a woman taking care of him, in marriage or through just living together, would benefit him financially and provide him with someone to clean his house, wash his clothes and cook for him.

During that time, disco was popular and he thought he was John Travolta. He walked like him, tried to talk like him, dressed like him, and, doubtless, tried to dance like him.

Greg drank a lot and saw nothing wrong with going out and not coming home for two or three days. After days of anguish on my part, he would stroll into the house just as happy as could be and say, "Good morning, Deborah." I would scream, yell, cry, plead, attempt to reason, threaten retaliation—nothing seemed to work. It was as if Greg was totally oblivious to how I felt, or worse, did not care. Even worse, after being gone three days, he would walk in and say, "Hey Deborah, what's for dinner?" "What do you mean, what's for dinner? I'm not cooking you any food." My rage would then escalate into a giant fit. He just seemed pleased as he could be that I was upset. Later, I learned the worse I acted, the more convinced he was that he was fully justified to come and go as he pleased.

I was determined to make the marriage work because I had never failed at anything and certainly was not going to fail in marriage. This was going to be the "perfect" household someday because I had made up my mind that it would be.

God gave me wisdom. There were times when Greg would be out until the wee hours of the morning and come home demanding breakfast. My refusals to cook would only result in an argument and my loss of sleep. One morning, I got up and started to boil water to cook rice when I discovered that by the time the water started to boil, Greg was asleep. I counted it as godly wisdom. I seldom had an argument or cooked breakfast ever again at that time of the morning. Boiling water did the trick.

In addition to the heartache I had from Greg going out all the time, I was constantly worried about keeping our money away from him. I can't tell you the number of times I changed checking accounts because I was trying to keep Greg away from money set aside to pay bills. In his mind, if he went to the bank and checked the balance, he could spend whatever funds were available for withdrawal at that time. He did not consider any outstanding checks or bills that needed to be paid. He would withdraw money for new rims, tires, suits, or whatever he desired. He even had the audacity to come home and show off his grand purchases. Greg would max out credit cards that were in my name at the finest stores in town, and then ask for extensions on credit lines that were based on my salary. This was during the time when he only had to prove he was my spouse to be automatically added to my accounts.

He would walk in wearing a new suit and ask me, "Deborah, so how do you like my new suit I bought today?" It did not matter to him that the rent was not paid, the power bill was not paid, and there was no food in the house. After awhile, I began wondering, "Is he insane? Is there something wrong with his thinking?" Finally, I got a clue and did not tell him where I was depositing the money.

Then, the women started calling. Some said, they did not know he was married, and they were sorry. Others acted pretty hostile and blamed me for Greg's infidelity, claiming that I did not support him. Some seemed so shocked and hurt that I would apologize to them for my husband's behavior that led them on. One woman in particular continued to call me looking for Greg until I finally told her, "I am sorry that Greg has led you on in this way, but since you don't know where he is and I don't know where he is, we can both assume that he is with another woman. I can tell you this, though, he will eventually end up back home. He always does."

I believe that in some way I was Greg's reality. He would pretend so much when he was out partying that he had to come home in order to find himself. When Greg was out and about, he pretended to be a promoter, a recruiter, or some other Hollywood-industry bigwig; when he came home, I reminded him that he was home and could stop pretending. He always did.

Chapter Three:
Pushed to the Feet of Jesus

The situation was much bigger than I could handle. Even through all this, I had no intention of giving up. I was convinced that sometime, sooner or later, he would come home for good. Again, this was going to be a happy home because I had made up my mind that it would be.

Three years of the heartache of trying to make it work on my own pushed me into finding some assistance. My impossible situation was beyond any help my friends could provide. After many tormenting months of waiting at the window and crying myself to sleep, I made a decision that I should be happy. When I made this decision, I was able to draw from my childhood upbringing of my mother regularly taking me to church. She had raised me to know that no one should direct my life because it is ultimately up to me to do that. She had often told me that my own thoughts would determine my level of happiness, and that I would ultimately be the one to decide if a life circumstance would push me down or propel me forward. One of her favorite quotes was, "nothing is either good or bad, it's how you think of it." In other words, I had to categorize everything that happened to me. My mom figured that if nothing else, you gain experience from a bad situation. In this, she had taught me that even if something seems bad, there must be a silver lining in it somewhere if you love and trust God. She often would repeat a particular scripture to me that became one of my favorites, "And we know that all things work together for good to them that love God, to them who are the called according to his purpose" (Rom. 8:28).

Three years had passed and things had to change. My grandmother, whom I loved very much had died, we had been evicted from our apartment and were living with Greg's parents, our car had been repossessed, I had lost my first child due to still-birth, and I had a husband who lived outside of reality. Things just had to change.

Initially, I had tried to do things on my own, thinking I was smart enough to change my circumstances and change my husband's heart, but over time, all the disappointment, frustration and stress caused me to realize that I needed God's help. I was not saved, but I wanted to be. I sought the Lord in my living room one night, desperate to gain some assurance that He would accept me and give me peace. I dropped all my social activities, even a social club my best friend and I had founded. I was too unhappy to even pretend. It was time to get some peace and be happy. Even I, who had once been so self-righteous, had come to realize that only God could give me the kind of peace I was looking for.

Greg stays out all night. Sometimes he stays out three days at a time. He comes home as though nothing has happened and expects me to act like everything's ok. What in the world am I going to do with this man?" Daily, I asked God this question after I had gotten saved and was assured of my own salvation. I was no longer vulnerable. As a matter of fact, I knew I could make it with or without Greg. I almost did not see the purpose of being married on paper only. I was self-sufficient and loved God. God had even blessed me with increases on my job, a new car and the ability to move out of Greg's parents' home.

All this, for some reason, looked suspicious to Greg, and he began accusing me of meeting men at the church, or worse, of having an affair with one of the deacons. A person carrying a lot of guilt tends to believe the worst about others. God, not an affair with another man, was supplying my needs and granting me favor in the midst of this mess. Some days, I would try to talk with Greg about church, but the more I talked to him about this, the more disinterested and cynical he became.

Soon after my salvation, I was pregnant again. Our son, Gregory Alexander was born October 8, 1980. Greg was so happy; he carried little Greg with him practically everywhere he went. He had a job but still went out nights. Fifteen months later, on January 29, 1982, Christopher Lamar was born. Greg was proud of having two sons and was still holding down a job. He was a little better at sharing the responsibility of paying the bills, but nightlife kept calling him. He even went to church to get saved, but became very discouraged when the training classes that the church offered were repeatedly cancelled. Pretty soon he slipped back into the partying lifestyle, only now it was worse.

I now had a personal relationship with God through Jesus Christ, but once again, I started making incorrect assumptions. I assumed that getting saved meant that God would straighten Greg out. I would learn, however, that there were no guarantees of this. Every individual is a free moral agent, and Greg could end up choosing through an act of free will to reject God.

Greg's life seemed to be spiraling down, headed towards disaster, and there was nothing I could do about it. I came to understand that Greg might never become the man I dreamed he could be, and my hope of a happy home might never be realized. I would have to learn to serve the Lord out of love for Jesus Christ, not as a means of straightening out my household. God would help me, but the focus of that help could not be on making Greg "behave."

I remember talking to God and telling Him how I wished it were

19

"me, You and Greg," but I had come to the realization that it was just "me and You, God." The first time I said this to God I felt so alone because it appeared that our marriage was over; but the more I said it, the stronger I became, because repeating this little prayer helped me realize and begin to experience that God was big enough to fill the void.

At the time I did not understand that God is a jealous God, and He will have no other gods before Him. He was leading me to place Him at the head of my heart.

Unsaved Husbands are Unsaved People

Romans 1:30 makes reference to people who are inventors of evil. This description reminds me of the days I spent with my husband when I was saved and he was not. When I read this scripture, I determined that he must be one of those being described in that passage as an "inventor of evil." Beginning just a few months after we were married, it seemed that the evil Greg knew was not enough for him, and he felt compelled to invent ever-increasing levels of sin and evil.

One day when I was particularly frustrated with this "inventor of evil," the Lord reminded me of a conversation I had once had with my mother. She had asked, "Deborah, does Greg do anything you are surprised about?" When I reluctantly answered "no," she had asked, "Then why are you flustered and upset when he does the expected?" After reminding me of this conversation, God spoke to me and said, "Unsaved people do what unsaved people do."

Why was I expecting otherwise? Why was I expecting him to act like a Christian when he was not? I was setting myself up for unnecessary disappointment. People in general tend to be disappointed with the unsaved loved ones who "won't act right." If we, on the other hand, do not expect an unsaved person to act saved, we cannot be disappointed when an unsaved person lies, drinks, smokes, parties or cheats. That person is not acting out of character.

Instead of reeling from the disappointment of having our illogical expectations unfulfilled, we can choose to understand the profile of the unsaved person and do our part to fast, pray, study the Word and witness. We can choose to intercede for them to come into the knowledge of the truth of the Word of God. That is exactly what I had to do concerning Greg. Days of peace would follow that revelation.

Temptation Knocks

When Satan starts cooking up a mess, he normally tries to at least double his damage. Knowing this firsthand, I would be negligent if I did not mention that he tried to tempt me to fall prey to infidelity as well. As Greg stayed out later and later, or was sometimes gone for days at a time, it seemed like other men started trying to snare me wherever I went. I hadn't experienced so much attention since my college days.

When my marital problems began to escalate, other men started saying things to me such as: "You're so pretty." "You're so cute." I became so angry with one man who made "cat-calls" after I had passed him in the mall that I turned around, walked back to where he and his friend were standing, and said, "Do you see this ring? This means, I am married. How would you like it if your wife or your girlfriend responded to some guy in the mall who was acting like you are?" I went on, "I am sure you would be pretty upset if she gave him the time of the day." He was embarrassed and apologized.

21

At my job, some of my customers tried to flirt with me over the phone. One client actually drove fifty miles to surprise me and take me to lunch. I refused to go. Some of Greg's so-called friends came by when they knew Greg was not home. I knew what they were up to and talked to them through the door rather than let them in.

I am sad to say that even a pastor approached me. I had been referred to him for counseling, but I began to feel uncomfortable after I had briefly talked with him over the phone just two or three times. Afterwards, he called me at work and told me, "If I were to commit adultery, I would do it with you."

What a horrible thing to say! I was stunned. Unfortunately, I was not in a position to say what I wanted to say even though I felt betrayed and very angry. Here I was trying to cope with one mess, and this pastor who was supposed to be doing the work of the Lord was trying to get me involved in another one.

He then showed up at my job the following day and asked me if he could take me to lunch. I refused. When he called a couple of days later, I told him that he had made me feel uncomfortable with his inappropriate comment and actions. I asked him not to call me again and warned him that I would tell my husband if he tried.

After this incident, I began to wonder how many women have fallen in similar circumstances. I now know that some women do fall prey to these antics of the devil, especially when their self-esteem is low and another man is telling them the things they wish their husbands would say.

It is important for women faced with these kinds of propositions to realize that the man is interested because being with a married woman would allow him to be free of any obligations. Also, any minister who tries to take advantage of a woman in this manner is in no position to help anyone and probably has more than one woman dangling in his web of lies and manipulation.

When this minister tried to rope me in, I got so upset and angry about it that I called my mother. She helped me work through this sting of disappointment. I advise any woman approached by a minister or counselor in this way to report his inappropriate behavior to his superiors immediately in order to protect other women from possible harm.

To Stay or Not to Stay

Very soon after I was saved, I faced the decision that every woman who is married to an unsaved man must face: Do you want this marriage? Will you stay with him or will you leave?

How could I possibly bring glory to God through my life by continuing in such a horrendous situation? My life reeked with the stench of my husband's sin. I prayed, "God, do you want me to leave this man? I know where the door is. I know how to walk away." As I prayed, I also determined that now that I was saved, I still wanted the marriage. I decided to stay because I wanted to stay, and because God did not tell me to leave. After sorting this out before the Lord, I prayed, "God, if you want me to stay, then please give me what I need to continue on because I cannot do this alone."

Avoiding the Naysayer

All along, many people around me had been disagreeing with my decision to stay with Greg. Because my mind was made up and I wanted to stay firm-footed in my determination to make our marriage work, I separated myself from those who were critical of my husband. I certainly did not need anyone to tell me what I already knew about him. I knew my decision seemed illogical, and arguing with other people would not get me anywhere.

Many friends warned me saying, "I wouldn't stay with him," or "I can't believe you are taking all of that," or "you shouldn't have to live with that." If I thought about it logically, I'd agree. Yet, I was still determined to make it work, and I figured it was truly possible now that I had God's help.

I tried to find people who supported my decision and would encourage me to believe for the best and most for my marriage. Very few people supported me in my decision. Many thought I should leave. I also found that most people were incapable of giving me advice that would build up my faith to endure what would be necessary to maintain my decision. My one or two supporters were, at best, only good listeners who were capable of just letting me talk.

Even though I had to accept that Greg might never change, I also began to receive hope that God would make him into the man I wanted him to be. The ability to air my grievances without criticism was a wonderful stress relief. Very few people knew the details of my marriage and that is the way I wanted it. I did, however, need a sounding board. Every once in awhile a dear friend, Audrey Jones, would remind me of Mark 10:29, "And Jesus answered and said, Verily I say unto you, There is no man that hath left house, or brethren, or sisters, or father, or mother, or wife, or children, or lands, for my sake, and the gospel's, but he shall receive an hundredfold now in this time, houses, and brethren, and sisters, and mothers, and children, and lands, with persecutions; and in the world to come eternal life." She would remind me that I must leave Greg at the feet of Jesus and allow Him to do the work.

My best friend Linda would just listen and encourage me. She kept me from becoming depressed and thinking it was all because of something that was wrong with me. She encouraged me to keep my appearance up and make plans to enjoy life. She took care of my children during the day and sometimes would keep them after working hours to give me time to go shopping, have my hair done, or do whatever would relax me.

My mom listened to me and encouraged me to just do what I believed God was saying. These three people gave me encouragement, but my comfort came from a deepening relationship with God. He was faithful to strengthen and comfort me in His love.

Staying, but Letting Go

In the early months and years after I accepted Jesus Christ as my Lord and Savior, my focus was on my husband changing. I sought for ways to change him myself, and I prayed continually, determined that God should be working on him too.

As I continued in my journey to get to know Jesus in a more personal way, I realized that God wanted me to take my focus off of trying to change my husband and instead begin working on myself. Rather than trying to control Greg, I was to pursue the change that needed to take place in me. This meant allowing the Word of God to renew me from the inside out and transform me into the person that He created me to be.

This pursuit was not unlike the time when David and his men

came back to their homes to find that their children, wives and possessions were gone. David asked the Lord if he should pursue their attackers and recover what had been stolen from them. The Lord's answer was, "Yes, pursue and recover all."

> *And David enquired at the LORD, saying, Shall I pursue after this troop? Shall I overtake them? And he answered him, Pursue: for thou shalt surely overtake them, and without fail recover all.*
>
> —1 Samuel 30:8

At first, I pursued the recovery of a TV sitcom image of marriage. Later, I pursued some sense of stability and normalcy. But now, I knew that I was to pursue a deep understanding of the Word of God and its power to change me.

It was obvious that the knowledge and ability to do things God's way was not just going to fall on me. I had to run after it. I had to mine the nuggets of truth in the Word, examine them before the Spirit of God in prayer, and invest their value in my life. For this to happen, I would have to put my most valued treasure—my marriage—into the hands of the Lord. I would need to let go and let God.

The Bible says, "The kingdom of heaven is like unto treasure hid in a field; which when a man hath found, he hideth, and for joy thereof goeth and selleth all that he hath, and buyeth that field" (Matt. 13:44). In order to accomplish the "letting go and letting God," the Father had to get my attention, and what He showed me hit me like a ton of bricks. One night, I was so very upset with Greg that I was in tears. I cried out to God, "What is going on; what is the problem? I am trying to do what

You say and nothing is changing."

I opened the Bible and let the pages fall where they may. The first place it opened, I thought, "That's not the answer." The second time I let if flop open, it landed on Proverbs 3:5, "Trust in the Lord with all thy heart; and lean not unto thine own understanding." I gazed at the scripture and cleared the tears from my eyes because deep down inside of me, I knew that was the answer. I said out loud, "God, is that what it is? Is it that I do not really trust You?"

I began to cry again, repenting before God for my not trusting Him, for asking Him for help and then not trusting that He would help me. What a hypocrite I had been. I got up from that time of repenting and told God, "I will trust You. No matter what I see, I will trust You."

Part II: Me and You, Lord, Make Two

Chapter Four:
Honoring God, Through Hardship

A key to my letting go of my efforts to control Greg's relationship with God was my realization that my motives were selfish. I wanted Greg to change in order to make my life better. In truth, I had little concern over Greg's salvation beyond seeing it as a means for making my life easier.

> *Lay not up for yourselves treasures upon earth, where moth and rust doth corrupt, and where thieves break through and steal: But lay up for yourselves treasures in heaven, where neither moth nor rust doth corrupt, and where thieves do not break through nor steal: For where your treasure is, there will your heart be also.*
>
> —Matthew 6:19-21

First, I had been asking God to straighten Greg up because I wanted him to become a good provider and father who went to church with his family. My prayer was: "God, You need to get him to act right. He needs to come home and provide for his family. He needs to get a good job, and he needs to go to church. And he needs to do this, this, this and this".

One time God interrupted my prayer concerning Greg with a question. He asked, "Would you be happy if Greg did those things but was still unsaved?" I replied, "But Lord, that's not what I meant." I could not argue when He said, "But that's what you are praying."

I had acted as if God "needed" me to tell Him what He "needed" to do. God's reply to this was, "Oh, so it doesn't matter to you if he goes to hell? All you want is for his behavior to change?" This was just the beginning of the challenge. He then told me, "You are really praying a selfish prayer. You want him to get right for you, when I need for him to get right for Me." This was the first step in my change in perspective.

My second step was my realization that my motive for wanting this was also rooted in pride. I did not want to fail in anything, including my marriage. My pride would not allow it. This had been my primary motive for wanting the marriage to work prior to my salvation, and it had continued to be my motive afterwards. I decided to look up all the scriptures concerning marriage and do them, saying to myself, that if this marriage breaks up, it will be all Greg's fault. I would have done my part, and no one could blame me if we broke up.

I had been fooling myself into thinking that I had selfless motives for wanting Greg to change. I realized that I had to start to love my husband as one that was lost and needed to know God—not for my benefit, but for his own. The time had come for me to take my eyes off myself and begin to have a more eternal perspective. This had not been possible prior to my salvation. Again, I had come to terms with the fact that unsaved husbands act like unsaved people, and I had to understand that my salvation would not save Greg. He had to make that decision to accept Jesus as Lord. As I continued to bring Greg before the Lord in prayer, I actually came to the point where I would pray for Greg's salvation because I wanted him to know God regardless of whether we were together. I finally was loving him with an unselfish love.

Now the end of the commandment is charity out of a pure heart, and of a good conscience, and of faith unfeigned"

—1 Timothy 1:5

As my perspective became less selfish and more eternal, I realized that Greg could make a great impact in the Body of Christ, and Satan was trying to stop this plan of God for Greg's life. When this happened, my focus shifted away from myself and towards the greater good. The understanding that my efforts were on behalf of the Kingdom of God, which in turn caused God to act on my behalf, encouraged me for the battle ahead.

I started to see my husband as someone who needed God and had a divine part in God's overall plan for mankind. That's when I placed God in the center of my marriage. Until then it was all about me. Now, I was letting go of being obsessed with my own desires and becoming more and more fixed on submitting myself to God and becoming the person God had called me to be in my marriage and in every other aspect of my life.

Stop Trying to Make Him Turn to God

Before I left Greg in God's hands, I had done everything I could think of to change him. Buying books and leaving them around the house did not work. Opening the Bible to passages I thought he needed to read and leaving it where he would come across them did not work either. If I had known about anointing oil back then, I probably would have anointed him in his sleep. I was quite desperate in my efforts in trying to play God, not realizing that only God can move on the heart of men.

Even if what I had said or the hints I had left around the house had convinced him to change some of his behaviors, the changes would have been only temporary if they were not from the heart. The kind of transformation he needed was the kind that did not rely on my ongoing manipulations; it would be possible only as he responded to God's drawing him towards eternal life. Only then could Jesus Christ completely transform his priorities, values and viewpoint.

Over time I learned that each person is responsible for his/her own relationship with God. God expected me to have, and to develop, my own relationship with Him. He also, in turn, expected Greg to have a relationship with Him, and I could not interfere with what God was doing in that relationship. Every morning I continued to wake up and start my prayer with, "It's me and You, God; and Greg is your business." I had to remind myself not to get involved.

Stop Trying to Change His Lifestyle

At this point, I had purer motives for wanting God to change Greg through salvation, and I had stopped trying to manipulate Greg into having a relationship with God. I continued to be very torn up about how Greg was living his life. I had become so acquainted with crying, fussing, screaming, having tantrums, and making threats to get back at him, that I thought my anger was what expressed my love. I was afraid that if I let up doing these things, my love would somehow go away, and I would have to give up on our marriage.

This assumption changed as I read the scripture: "And the peace of God, which passeth all understanding, shall keep your hearts and minds through Christ Jesus" (Phil. 4:7). I knew that was what I wanted and needed. Right then and there, I told God, "That's what I want. I want peace that surpasses all understanding."

My anger was not doing either of us any good. It was not bringing about any change of heart in him, and it was driving me into a frenzy. It was not easy for me to come to grips with the fact that walking in peace, rather than in anger, was an authentic expression of love. In many ways, it was the real starting place in my working on me rather than on my husband. I had to stop fussing and be calm.

> *Wherefore, my beloved brethren, let every man be swift to hear, slow to speak, slow to wrath: For the wrath of man worketh not the righteousness of God.*
>
> —James 1:19-20

At first, this was a hard scripture for me because I did not want to feel like I was being taken advantage of. I wanted Greg to know I was aware of the things he did and that I was not an "airhead". I would, upon occasion, walk through the house and ask him, "What is your new girlfriend's name," and before he could answer, I would say, "That's all right, I don't want to know." I had to stop being so sarcastic.

There were times when I would hear him pulling in the driveway, and I would go to the bathroom and repeat over and over again: slow to speak, quick to hear, and slow to anger. I conquered my mouth most of the time. Every once in a while, I would start to lose control of my tongue but would catch myself. Sometimes in the middle of a conversation, I would have to take a break to go into the bathroom to remind myself to stay in control. At other times, I told God everything I was thinking about Greg and was then able to return to the conversation

35

calm.

The peace that came did not suggest an end to my hardship. Neither did it suggest the end of trouble. Peace is the presence of God in the midst of difficulties. Peace is wholeness, nothing missing, nothing lacking, and nothing broken because peace is ours when we dwell in Christ Jesus. In God's peace, we lack nothing because we are now of the family and Kingdom of God, and all that is good is ours by faith.

According to Thayer and Smith's KJV New Testament Greek Lexicon, within the context of the Christian life, the Greek word for peace, kurieuo, is defined as "the tranquil state, of a soul assured of its salvation through Christ, and so fearing nothing from God and content with its earthly lot, of whatsoever sort that is." Peace in God would be mine, and in this tranquil state I no longer feared that God was not on my side. I found contentment despite my current circumstances. My determination to have peace regardless of my circumstances is what brought me to the place that I was able to remain tranquil even when my husband was on his way out the door for another night, or two, or three on the town. I sometimes told Greg how good he looked and to have a good time. During one conversation, he told me he was happy and was enjoying life. I did not believe him, but I told him if he thought he was happy then that was what was important. I became so free and peaceful, only God could have accomplished that in me.

Knowing I could not do anything to change his choices, I began to view his disappearances as a time for me to really study the Bible. To keep myself from being distracted from peace and pure thoughts as Greg walked out the door, I asked God to let me know if Greg got himself into a physically dangerous situation. I prayed, "If he is in any trouble, just let me know so I can pray him through it because we want him to be saved before he dies."

> *Finally, brethren, whatsoever things are true, whatsoever things are honest, whatsoever things are just, whatsoever things are pure, whatsoever things are lovely, whatsoever things are of good report; if there be any virtue, and if there be any praise, think on these things.*
>
> —Philippians 4:8

Over the Long Haul

The path Greg was on seemed so dangerous that I increased the life insurance on him to the maximum the policy allowed, because I thought there was a good chance that he would not live much longer at the "crazy" rate he was going.

Although I was concerned about my husband's safety, I did not allow myself to be consumed by worry. At each step in living in God's peace, I gave Greg to God while at the same time hoping for a godly marriage. From where we were, this was a giant leap of faith, but I was firm; I wanted this marriage and I wanted it to work, in spite of what it looked like at the time.

To keep from worrying, I had to cleave to my belief that God was greater than any demon who would try to take Greg's life before he became a Christian. I did not see any way in which God seemed to be working on Greg's behalf, other than keeping him alive. I saw no change whatsoever.

When fear would begin to creep in, I would have to choose to see God as bigger than the dangers Greg was facing in any given moment. It was like putting a magnifying glass on God so that all that could be seen was how large God is. I brought this magnifying glass to all that I knew about the goodness of God and to His promises to the believer. By making a conscious effort to do this whenever the fears and doubts came knocking on my mind, any possible plot of the enemy seemed to have lost its power to bring fear to my heart.

I did not realize it at the time, but by doing this, I was glorifying God in spite of my circumstances. I was making the choice to have faith that God was in control and more than able to keep my mind fixed on Him while He was working our situation out.

Glorifying God through my present circumstances also meant that I did not esteem my desire to have a good marriage above my desire to please God. I had put God first by surrendering this desire to God and allowing Him to purify my motives for wanting Greg to be saved. By no longer trying to manipulate Greg into becoming a Christian, I was also glorifying God by releasing control of Greg to Him. He was guiding me to place Him, rather than my own desires, on the throne of my heart.

It was certainly not easy to stay fixed in faith with my focus on God, but as I did this, Greg became less and less of an "idol" to me. God was using my ungodly circumstances to shape me and make me more like Jesus every day.

Even now, I draw upon this experience when faced with a temptation to allow the appearance of present circumstances to pull me away from faith in healing or in the truth of a revelation that I have received for myself or for another person. Today, when people say things contrary to the Word of God, or what I know the Lord has revealed to me, I draw on my past experiences with God and magnify Him. I esteem Him as much larger than the circumstances I'm facing.

Magnifying God in this way is what kept me from changing my mind about seeing my marriage succeed. God had not told me to leave, and now He was giving me the wisdom, strength and faith to continue on in Him despite my circumstances.

Chapter Five:
Submitting to an Unsaved Husband

With this new view of myself and of my husband, my motives were pure enough for me to become a submitted wife—even with an unsaved husband. My next step in yielding my life to God was to become a submitted wife to my unsaved husband.

Being Obedient without Knowing God's "Whys"

Being obedient to the Word of God often requires us to receive by faith what we do not yet understand with our minds or see with our eyes.

> *Lean on, trust in, and be confident in the Lord with all your heart and mind and do not rely on your own insight or understanding.*
>
> —Proverbs 3:5 AMP

We really do not need to understand all of the "whys" for doing something the Bible tells us to do. Many people believe that not understanding why God requires them to do something is a justification for delaying their obedience. Often, this is because they feel they need to agree with God before obeying Him. This is actually a form of glorifying one's own opinions above God's Word. The truth of God's Word and the requirement for us to obey is simply not dependent upon it making sense to our natural mind to the point where we agree with it.

Obeying without understanding the "whys" is an act of faith that glorifies God. For women, this is often true when it comes to submission in marriage.

> *Wives, submit yourselves unto your own husbands, as unto the Lord.*
>
> —Ephesians 5:22

> *Wives, submit yourselves unto your own husbands, as it is fit in the Lord.*
>
> —Colossians 3:18

Submission must occur even before a woman fully understands the reasons why God would have her submit to her husband because it seems so contrary to Western culture. I have found that in this area and in other areas the "whys" are revealed over time, as the fruits of the obedience become evident.

This meant in order to move forward in my walk with the Lord, my attitude toward my husband and my relationship with him needed to change. I needed to have a "voluntary attitude of giving in, cooperating, assuming responsibility, and carrying a burden." To be a godly helper to my husband, I would need to take on an humble attitude of compliance, cooperation and helpfulness. This position of being a helper had been ordained when God created the first woman, Eve. "Now the Lord God said, It is not good (sufficient, satisfactory) that the man should be alone; I will make him a helper meet (suitable, adapted, complementary) for him" (Gen., 2:18, AMP). Over time, it would also bring me added peace, but initially it would be very hard for me to receive because I did not consider that Greg "deserved" this kind of treatment.

It was clear to me that this submission to him did not mean that I joined him in his lifestyle of sin. There were many things I could do to fulfill this requirement without joining him in sin. For starters, I could focus on being a good wife to him, rather than on my desire for him to be a good husband to me. When I determined I would obey God in this area, the Lord showed me more and more ways for me to do this. I complimented him at every opportunity, regardless of where he was going. I made sure he had dinner, whether he ate it or not. I made sure his clothes were clean, whether he ever thanked me or not. My motive was love for him and for God. My submission to him was a form of submission to God.

When I began to understand that I was to submit to Greg as my husband, I thought about something God had shown me when I made the decision to stay with Greg after I was saved. At that time, God had shown me through the book of Philippians that I was not to complain about my situation. At that time, it had been a form of protecting me from the natural tendency to solicit advice from people who did not agree with my decision to stay with Greg. It had also helped me to not wallow even more in negativity.

Not only was I to submit to Greg, but I had to reverence him as well. This meant I had to notice him, regard him, honor him, prefer him, venerate him, esteem him, defer to him, praise him, love him, and admire him exceedingly, according to Eph. 5:33, AMP. At first this would seem hard, but God will not require you to do something you are unable to do without His help. At this time, it thrilled me to see God's Word working. Greg had not changed, but my thinking had changed tremendously.

Saved People are to Only Marry Saved People

I warn women not to use my testimony as an excuse to run out and marry an unsaved man. First, she will be going against all she knows to be true, including the scriptural admonition for Christians not to be unequally yoked together with unbelievers. "Be ye not unequally yoked together with unbelievers: for what fellowship hath righteousness with unrighteousness? And what communion hath light with darkness?" (2 Cor. 6:14).

Second, I tell them that the woman who makes the decision to do this will be in an even worse situation than mine. I was unsaved when I married an unsaved man. On the other hand, being saved and marrying someone who is unsaved would be a willful act of disobedience that would be a choice to fulfill the lust of the flesh and would surely yield dire consequences.

> *Wherein in time past ye walked according to the course of this world, according to the prince of the power of the air, the spirit that now worketh in the children of disobedience: Among whom also we all had our conversation in times past in the lusts of our flesh, fulfilling the desires of the flesh and of the mind; and were by nature the children of wrath, even as others. But God, who is rich in mercy, for his great love wherewith he loved us, Even when we were dead in sins, hath quickened us together with Christ, (by grace ye are saved;) And hath raised us up together, and made us sit together in heavenly places in Christ Jesus.*
>
> —Ephesians 2:2-6

The Wife's Role in Marriage

Even though I wanted my marriage to be all that the Word of God said it should be, I realized I really had not looked in the Word of God to see what marriage really was supposed to be like. My picture of the perfect marriage was still primarily based upon what I had seen on TV and in movies, what I had read in books, and what I had heard other people say. I had never investigated what the Word of God said about marriage.

My analysis of this began with a study of the wife's responsibilities according to the Bible. Although my research was motivated by pride, I would find that my desire to be obedient to God would allow Him to steer me to the right course and also purify my motives. I must say that I was very upset about those responsibilities because I thought they were unfair, especially when compared to those of the husband. It seemed to me that the wife's list of responsibilities was much longer than the husband's. In fact, I could not find a list for him. All I could find was that he was to love his wife as Christ loves the church. "Husbands, love your wives, even as Christ also loved the church, and gave himself for it" (Eph. 5:25).

I would later come across another key scripture that addresses husbands. "Likewise, ye husbands, dwell with them according to knowledge, giving honour unto the wife, as unto the weaker vessel, and as being heirs together of the grace of life; that your prayers be not hindered" (1 Pet. 3:7).

Of course, over time I would learn that the husband loving his wife as Christ loved the Church was much more involved. Christ laid down his life for the Church, gave up power and position in heaven and came down as a servant. This passage meant a husband would need to die to his selfish desires in order to love her.

I would also learn that the husband dwelling with the wife according to knowledge and giving honor to her as unto the weaker vessel was also very deep in meaning and rich in responsibility. At this point, God was keeping me focused on the work He was doing in me, not on my husband.

I even closed the Bible immediately after reading, the passage of scripture where Sarah called Abraham "lord." "Even as Sarah obeyed Abraham, calling him lord: whose daughters ye are, as long as ye do well, and are not afraid with any amazement" (1 Pet. 3:6). After shutting the Bible, I replied, "Jesus is Lord, not Greg Powe." But I had to open the Bible back up. At the time, I did not understand what was meant by Sarah calling him "lord." I did not realize that this was a sense of reverence and respect rather than a form of worship of a man. Eventually God made this clear to me.

While it is true that I was not to worship Greg as an "idol" or in the way that I would worship my Lord and Savior Jesus Christ, I was to honor him as the head of our home and father of our children.

I would like to again emphasize just how out of God's order it is for a saved woman to marry an unsaved man. If she does this, she will be choosing the desires of the flesh over the things of the Spirit, and she will be subjecting herself to having an unsaved man as lord over her and as her master in her marriage.

Stop Arguing

As I studied what the scriptures had to say about the role of the wife, God was really working on my attitude toward my husband once again. Not only was I to continue to fulfill my responsibilities as a wife even though he was not fulfilling his responsibilities as a husband, but along with this, I was to stop arguing with him. Now that I better understood my role as a wife, I was to once again stop complaining about how unfair it was for me to have to continue holding up my end even though he certainly was not "loving me as Christ loved the Church."

When God revealed these next pieces of the puzzle to me, I had already discovered that arguing with an unsaved person is pointless. The logic and strength of my case made absolutely no difference when I argued with him. I always found myself being dragged through the muck of Greg's confused values, and in the end, we would have traveled down one bunny trail after another and made absolutely no headway toward him accepting, or even recognizing, the validity of my perspective and reasoning. Instead, I usually was the one who was left looking like the "bad guy" because I was frustrated about not being able to make my point, and Greg was as happy as could be about pulling off another escape from taking responsibility or accepting the need for change.

Greg told me later that it really ate at him when I started to act in line with the Word. He told me he felt helpless, like he had no more justification for his behavior. He was trying hard to start arguments with me because he was running out of ammunition and would have to admit he was just wrong if he could no longer find fault in me.

After I understood that God did not want me to argue with Greg anymore, I began to come across scriptures like: "Give not that which is holy unto the dogs, neither cast ye your pearls before swine, lest they trample them under their feet, and turn again and rend you" (Matt. 7:6).

I also understood more clearly how important it was for me to exhibit the fruit of the Spirit at all times in my home. "But the fruit of the Spirit is love, joy, peace, longsuffering, gentleness, goodness, faith, meekness, temperance" (Gal. 5:22-23). I also knew Philippians 1:6, "Being confident of this very thing, that he which hath begun a good work in you will perform it until the day of Jesus Christ."

With practice, I learned more ways to keep from falling into traps that would distract me from following "after righteousness, godliness, faith, love, patience, meekness, fight the good fight of faith, and lay hold on eternal life", (1 Tim. 6:11-12 rephrased). When I made a mistake and fell back into my old ways of responding to Greg's antics, Satan would try to make me feel inadequate as a Christian and unworthy of the promises of God.

When this happened, I had to stand on the fact that my adequacy was in Jesus Christ, and it was only through Him that I was worthy of God's promises anyway. I would apologize to Greg and to God and ask for their forgiveness. No matter how many times I fell into the snare of being frustrated and showing it, I would turn from my old ways once again and ask God to help me overcome. Eventually, it became easier and easier as I allowed God to give me peace that surpasses all understanding.

Over time, my outbursts became less frequent. By pursuing righteousness and holding fast to the grace of God, I was more confident in my position of having Christ's authority over sin and being free from its penalties.

There is therefore now no condemnation to them which are in Christ Jesus, who walk not after the flesh, but after the Spirit.

—Romans 8:1

While it would have been easy to become self-righteous about my decision and efforts not to argue with Greg anymore, I was humbled when I saw myself in the proverb, "It is better to live in a corner of a roof than in a house shared with a contentious woman" (Prov. 21:9, NAS). For three years, I had been that woman, and for three years, Greg had used my contentiousness as his excuse for leaving the house for days on end. By obeying God in this, Greg would have to walk out the door without having his old excuses to fall back on.

Chapter Six:

Being Happy During Hardship

In all the misery he was causing me, my husband did not seem to be the least bit unhappy. In fact, he seemed quite content. I was seeking God and should have enjoyed peace and happiness. But often I felt at my wit's end—frustrated, angry, and sometimes defeated. After facing this fact, I decided to change. I told the Lord, "Ok, if he's going to be happy, I need to be happy too."

> *Rejoice evermore. Pray without ceasing. In every thing give thanks: for this is the will of God in Christ Jesus concerning you.*
> —1 Thessalonians 5:16-18

I'd been deeply unhappy since the first month of my marriage. I barely knew what it meant to feel happy anymore. I wondered, "How do I get to the place where I am happy?"

I knew that putting on a façade of happiness was not the answer. Pretending to be happy would be going back to putting on a show for others like I had done before I was saved. I knew that my life experience of being married to Greg during those early years had forced me to get to know God for real and to face my own character flaws. For me, there was no turning back.

Reflecting on my own quest to be happy during that period of time reminds me of other women I've met over the years who became dissatisfied after they were saved but their husbands were not. I have heard such women facing this situation anew say, "Now that I'm born

51

again, my husband is irritated about the time I'm spending studying the Bible and praying. He doesn't like me coming to church, and he doesn't want me giving tithes and offerings. I don't know how I'm going to put up with this."

To the woman who lists these kinds of complaints, I usually say something like, "Neither of you were saved when he married you. Now, instead of doing the things together that you used to do, you are reading the Bible, praying and going to church. He is unable to identify with you. He probably feels like he has lost you, and is in competition with someone for your affection that he can not see."

To the woman who indicates to me that she is neglecting her husband because she has redirected her time and attention in this way, I suggest that she return to attending to her husband and giving him the attention that a wife should give her husband. I tell her that it is important for her to not set her husband up to resent the time she spends with the Lord. Instead, he should be drawn to the Lord by her love and care for him. She should become the wife noted in the scriptures who seeks how she may please her husband in everything that is right.

> *Likewise, ye wives, be in subjection to your own husbands; that, if any obey not the word, they also may without the word be won by the conversation of the wives.*

> —1 Peter 3:1

(The conversation in this scripture means, your manner of life or behavior.)

She should seek the Lord for wisdom and choose a study and prayer time that will not conflict with her time with her husband. The book of James tells us to ask for wisdom. She may have to get up a little earlier, stay up a little late, or use her lunch break for her time with God. Twenty years ago, God set my time for this at 5:30 a.m. From time to time, I have tried to change it, but it still works out best for me at 5:30 a.m.

To the woman who complains that she is frustrated because her husband has not accepted Jesus as Lord and will not change his lifestyle, I also suggest that she go home and apologize to her husband for trying to change him. In these cases, the woman is usually completely shocked and puzzled. When she asks me why she should be the one to apologize, I say, "Because you are the one who changed. He doesn't know who you are. Neither of you were saved when he married you. One day he came home and found a different woman than the one he married, and along with this, the new woman is now completely dissatisfied with who he is and is hounding him to change everything about himself and his life."

I tell the woman that it is selfish for her to be mad at him for being the person he has always been. She is the one who changed and turned his home and life upside down. I warn her that rejecting him through efforts to change him will only drive him away from her and away from the Lord. In most of these cases, the woman needs to go home and apologize to her husband for trying to force him to be a different person from the one she married. She usually, also needs to explain to him the fact that she now loves God does not change the fact that she also loves him and this will enhance their relationship and not hurt it.

In both of these kinds of situations, the woman will need to promise the husband that she will give him the attention he needs as a husband and pledge to attend to him even better, now that she loves the Lord. This is a good time for the woman to tell her husband that she believes there are some places where she does not believe God would want her to go and some things He would not want her to do, but the time they spend together going other places or doing other things will make their relationship stronger than ever. Telling him that now she needs fellowship with God, but that she will be even more attentive to him than ever before, will go a long way in initiating his support of this new life she now lives.

I am speaking from the voice of experience. I, too, had been quite self-righteous. In my quest to happily fulfill my role as a godly wife even in the midst of my circumstances, I had to come down from my high horse of self-righteousness from where I had been shouting to our housetop, "I'm so right and you are so wrong." I had to recognize that I had also had a part in the rift in the marriage. I knew what some of his tendencies were when I married him. They just seemed more exaggerated because I was now living with him. I, like most women thought marriage would change him.

Many women I have spoken to over the years, who are facing similar experiences, have seemed surprised by the fact that God will first begin working on them rather than on their husbands. They are surprised that His response to their cries for help often comes in the form of Him calling them to change their own attitudes and behaviors. As I listen to their stories while looking back over my own life, I see that it is actually quite logical for God to give guidance and direction to the person who is asking for help even though she thinks "fixing" her husband will "fix" all of her problems. In summation, God says to us, "Your husband was not the one who came to me. You did, so I am going to start with you."

For as the heavens are higher than the earth, so are my ways higher than your ways, and my thoughts than your thoughts.
—Isaiah 55:9

He Does Not Seem to Deserve It

Greg was a master at shifting the blame for his inconsistencies and shrugging responsibilities. In the beginning, I even helped him to do this because I wanted to believe the best about him. At first, I agreed that his plights on the job were everyone's fault except his; but then I realized that most of what was happening with Greg was largely because of choices he had made. I almost became belligerent when he offered me an excuse. I was losing respect for my husband. The thrill was gone, and I did not see much about him that I could respect and honor.

His financial decisions were getting ridiculous. They did not make any kind of sense. Greg had an engine replaced in our car and was to make the payments over time. The payments were only twenty dollars a month, but he would not make the payments, and as usual, I started making the payments for him.

Then when God blessed me with the ability to get a new car, I stopped making payments. My thinking was that if Greg is refusing to pay twenty dollars for a vehicle, then I will stop making payments as well. This did not get me far, though, because one day I went to the bank to cash a twenty-dollar check and discovered that our account had been frozen because we had stopped making payments. They would not give me one dime. I had deposited a $2,500 bonus check but could not withdraw any of it because the bank was in the process of returning all my checks until the matter was cleared. A bank teller, who knew me well, pulled me aside and told me what was happening. I returned to work and could not contain myself. When one of my coworkers heard me crying and tried to console me, I told her I would be all right. After praying and asking God what to do, I called the bank and pointed out that I had been paying regularly and had only skipped a couple of months. Favor kicked in and they released the account. Situations like this made honoring and reverencing Greg very difficult, especially when I saw how negatively his behavior could affect me if I let it happen.

Every time it appeared things were getting better, Greg would somehow manage to sabotage the progression. It was almost like he was afraid of success. Perhaps he was afraid he could not maintain the level of accomplishment he had risen to, so he would quit before he had a chance to fail. Even if I wanted to admire his successes, they were always so short-lived that it got to the point where I did not expect anything from Greg for fear of being let down yet again. I had to ask God to help me find something admirable about Greg.

At first, the only thing I could see was that he was a good dresser. Before I submitted to God, I would not compliment him on his style of dress because I was upset that he was not working and was spending the money I earned. However, he was, and is, a sharp dresser. This was something I could admire about him if I could look past the money issue that was tied to it at that time.

Also, he always bought toys and clothes for the boys. Sometimes, he would say that for the price of a case of beer, he could buy something for the boys. When he did, I could appreciate him for that. The list became progressively longer: not huge, but enough to help me start to change my attitude.

Respecting him while he was drinking, however, was a challenge because Greg drank from the morning to the evening. He would have a beer for breakfast, drink several for lunch, more on his way home, and then go out drinking in the evenings. Even though Greg was a functioning alcoholic, he never did lose a job because of his drinking. He also never brought his drinking friends to our home. For Greg, that was out of the question. He would go other places to drink with people, but there was very little, if any, alcohol in our home. God showed me that I could respect him for that.

There were things I could respect that were tied to the fact that Greg never wanted to do the ordinary stuff. His way was that if you must do something, you might as well do something different and exciting. This perspective spilled over into family time, and we indeed would have a good time. I just had to appreciate the time spent together and not focus on anything other than what was happening at the time. Our outings would be going to professional car races or riding with a motorcycle club from one state to another. Our picnics would never be at beaches near our home in Alabama. We would have to go to Biloxi, Mississippi or Pensacola, Florida. For family vacations, we would drive to different states and tour the historical areas of the cities. Greg would have researched the different cities before we traveled and would inform me of all the interesting facts about the city. Greg was and is very knowledgeable and would frequently go to the library to read about different places and things of interest to him. I could respect Greg for his creativity in planning family outings, and I could compliment him about his knowledge of different areas we visited.

Submitting to Greg was a whole other "ball of wax". I could not see the wisdom in "submitting to him" since he was the one who seemed to be making all the "stupid" decisions. This took time and I really did not submit to all of his ideas and choices until after he was born again.

One time, he wanted me to go "clubbing" with him, stating that he would not be prone to be with other women if his wife was present.

The first and only time I went to a club after salvation, I ran into two young ladies I had been witnessing to and lost all my credibility with them the minute they saw me there. I never went back to a nightclub after that and had to pray that someone else would cross their paths to lead them to salvation. Later, I would learn that a wife only submits to those things that are right.

Through tears, sometimes I obeyed the scripture concerning giving due benevolence to your spouse, (see 1 Corinthians 7:3). I hated this because I figured he had already had sex with someone else, so he need not bother me. During that day and time, there was not much talk about fatally transmitted diseases, so I submitted in ignorance. I thank God He protected me. Greg told me years later, he believed he had contracted a disease and thought he had passed it on to me. He told me he fervently prayed to God that it would never affect me and that God would cure him. I never experienced any repercussions of that disease.

During this day and time, I would advise any woman to make sure she hears from God concerning this area. If your faith is not strong enough to believe God that you will never contract a disease, take every necessary precaution to protect yourself.

As time went on, it became easier and easier to submit to Greg, but only in those things that were right. When I realized that respecting my husband's position as husband and father of our children was my duty before God, my anger and complaints about how unfair it all was started to dissipate.

Also, my frustration with Greg decreased when I stopped trying to assess whether he deserved my respect. The frequency of our arguments dwindled when I stopped trying to prove him wrong. Most of the time, Greg was not around when a decision had to be made, so there really was no point in fussing with him about a decision that would ultimately be made by me anyway.

These changes were combined with the fact that I displayed less hostility and anger when he went out or did things which I disagreed with. The key to my happiness was accepting and fitting into God's blueprint for marriage. As the frustration lifted, happiness took its place.

Exhibiting the Fruit of the Spirit

Rather than telling Greg that I had decided to be happy, I expressed my desire for him to be happy. Of course, he would never admit that he wasn't happy.

My approach to wanting Greg to be happy was unsettling for him. Without my chronic contentiousness, irritation, argumentativeness, complaining, and general state of unhappiness, he found fewer excuses for going out to party. At one point, he admitted that provoking me to anger made him feel better because then I didn't appear to be so "holy".

It is amazing how God can use some of the worst circumstances to prompt growth in a Christian. Not that God wants us to have such challenges, but we sometimes find ourselves in very stringent circumstances because of wrong choices or general life situations that emerge. When this happens, we may rest in Jesus' words: "In the world ye shall have tribulation: but be of good cheer; I have overcome the world" (Jn. 16:33). The Amplified Version expounds the scripture in this way, "In the world you have tribulation and trials and distress and frustration; but be of good cheer [take courage; be confident, certain, undaunted]! For I have overcome the world. [I have deprived it of power to harm you and have conquered it for you.]"

We may also find comfort in the scripture, "Many are the afflictions of the righteous: but the LORD delivereth him out of them all" (Psalm 34:19).

In spite of how life was for me at the time, God was at work building my character as a Christian. He was using the conditions I was in to prepare me for my future. When we are born again of the Spirit, the Holy Spirit produces the fruit of love, joy, peace, longsuffering, kindness, goodness, faithfulness, gentleness, and self-control in us. This fruit was being produced in me as I allowed the Holy Spirit to control my life. The first three in the list deal with our attitude towards God. The second three have to do with our social relationships and the last three describe principles that guide a Christian's conduct. I believe that the Father will use any test or trial to build His character in us.

I needed character. For example, if God was not first in my life, how could I have the love of God in my heart? Without that unselfish love, how could I properly love anyone else? Since the joy of the Lord gives a person strength, my joy had to come from what I knew about God rather than from what I was seeing and experiencing. This was closely dependent upon God showing me that I needed to trust Him. If I believed God was going to deliver me, why wouldn't I rejoice? I could rejoice even though I had not yet been delivered. That did not mean I was happy with the circumstances, but I could be happy while I was in the circumstances. I could also rejoice about the many things that happened to me that made me happy. In spite of Greg's behavior, I had purchased a new car, bought new clothes, received wage increases, purchased stock, had two beautiful children, and best of all, I had learned to trust God during these seven horrific years.

Because I was settled in the joy of knowing that God was for me,

I had peace. Not peace that was the result of the absence of trouble, but rather, peace that was the result of the presence of God being with me in the midst of the trouble. Also, through knowing that God was present and working on my behalf, I could have patience. I was allowing patience to have its perfect work. I knew that in accordance with scripture, I also would have want for nothing. This meant that I did not have to be overly anxious for anything while I waited on the timing of God.

I also learned that there is no excuse for bad behavior or unkindness. I did not have to take out my revenge on Greg. In Romans 12:19, God says, "Vengeance is mine; I will repay." I did not need to get in God's way. His motives were, and are, purer than mine. He wants to draw people to repentance. I, on the other hand, just wanted Greg to hurt like I was hurting.

God was telling me to be good to someone who was not being good to me. I had to act on behalf of Greg's best interest whether I thought he deserved it or not.

The Joy of the Lord

To appoint unto them that mourn in Zion, to give unto them beauty for ashes, the oil of joy for mourning, the garment of praise for the spirit of heaviness; that they might be called trees of righteousness, the planting of the LORD, that he might be glorified.

—Isaiah 61:3

In response to my cry, God was giving me wisdom about my role as a wife and then began to open my understanding to passages in

Scripture that would bring me added joy. For example, He began opening my eyes to whom I am in Christ and to His promises for me. He also revealed aspects of His character that helped me to see that He is more than able to care for me.

When I began my journey in fulfilling my decision to be happy, I did not realize that one of the byproducts would be that I would gain strength. "For this day is holy unto our Lord: neither be ye sorry; for the joy of the LORD is your strength" (Neh. 8:10).

Pressing into the fact that God had already given me everything that pertains to life and godliness (see 2 Peter 1:3). I would need strength to finish my course. Like Paul, I would be pressing forward and fulfilling the plan of God for my life with joy. "But none of these things move me, neither count I my life dear unto myself, so that I might finish my course with joy, and the ministry, which I have received of the Lord Jesus, to testify the gospel of the grace of God" (Acts 20:24).

It was in the midst of these changes in me and in my home that I also found another way to glorify the Lord. Unlike the many people who do not know to tithe, I welcomed the opportunity to honor God in yet another way. To have a godly attitude toward tithing required that I have a proper relationship with money. This begins with recognizing that the love of money is the root of all sorts of evil.

> *For the love of money is a root of all sorts of evil, and some by longing for it have wandered away from the faith and pierced themselves with many griefs.*
>
> —1 Timothy 6:10, NAS

While I did have my own struggles in other areas of obedience to

God, tithing was not one of them. Although I had been struggling with fear over not having enough money because of the decisions that Greg was making, I knew in my heart that God would make a way even where there seemed no way for us to tithe and still make ends meet. I made a decision to tithe because I wanted to do something to show God my love for Him.

> *Honour the LORD with thy substance, and with the firstfruits of all thine increase.* —*Proverbs 3:9*

Initially, I did not know that tithing was a vehicle through which God blessed His people. In the early days of reading the Bible, sometimes I did not read the scriptures above or below the one that answered a question that I wanted answered. So initially, I was only focused on the word "honor."

The churches I had attended in the past only spoke of their struggles and how God needed to help them. They even sang songs whining about their situations. God already knew my situation, and as far as I could understand, He wanted to help me and was helping me. Therefore, I wanted to do something that would make Him happy.

It was several years later that I found out about the blessing of being a tither. I did not actually understand what the churches were teaching about tithing at the time; I just started tithing to please God.

> *Bring ye all the tithes into the storehouse, that there may be meat in mine house, and prove me now herewith, saith the LORD of hosts, if I will not open you the windows of heaven, and pour you out a blessing, that there shall not be room enough to receive it.*
> —*Malachi 3:10*

Even in my ignorance, God started blessing me by honoring His Word and providing for my needs. I needed my family healed, and ultimately, that is just what I got. I needed financial healing, and over time, with patience, we were delivered in that area also. We discovered that the course of bad decisions may require a longer time before total manifestation of a promise from God is revealed. While it is true that God can work a miracle and bring someone out in one day, some things require knowledge and practice for the deliverance to be maintained. We had to both gain some financial knowledge and basic principles of budgeting and systematic saving. We had to learn how not to be consumers, but investors.

Chapter Seven:
Learning to Trust the Lord - No Matter What

As I stated earlier, trusting God and not the things I could accomplish in my own power was what triggered the beginning of a true relationship with God.

I wished I could describe the light, the warmth, and the joy that flooded my soul that night when I began to trust God—no matter what. The waves of different emotions that came that night were almost like a cleansing. I felt free and consumed with the love of God. It was like a burden was lifted just like He promised in the scripture:

> Come unto me, all ye that labour and are heavy laden, and I will give you rest. Take my yoke upon you, and learn of me; for I am meek and lowly in heart: and ye shall find rest unto your souls. For my yoke is easy, and my burden is light.

> —Matthew 11:28-30

I was ready to trust God because I truly had come to the end of myself. It would have been easy to just leave Greg, but I still would have had to one day come to this point of either trusting in God or in myself. Leaving Greg might have delayed my coming to this crossroads, but I believe that one way or another, I would have had to come to this point in my walk with the Lord.

As I mentioned earlier, there were three people in my life that I believe God used to help me make the decision to trust God even if my circumstances changed drastically.

One person was Audrey Jones, who was so kind to listen to me anytime of the day or night. Some Sundays after church, I would just sit at her house for about an hour because I simply did not want to go home. We would not talk about anything in particular at first, but eventually she would talk about the goodness of God and His ability to see me through tough times. I would be encouraged and go home. From time to time, she would have to remind me to leave Greg in the hands of God. She never once criticized Greg or anything I told her about what he did. Sometimes, she just shook her head and said, "He'll be all right; we are just going to keep praying for him. He'll change." Perhaps she knew this scripture that I did not know at the time: "Behold, the LORD's hand is not shortened, that it cannot save; neither his ear heavy, that it cannot hear" (Isaiah 59:1).

Again, I thank God for my mother as well. She was placed in an awkward position. Although she did not want to see me unhappy, she had made a decision when I got married that she would not interfere in my marriage. She told me that she would be there if I needed her help, but she was not going to live my life for me. She respected my decision to stay with Greg and gave me counsel about my attitude when it was in conflict with my decision to stay. I am sure she would have never been in agreement with this if I were in any physical danger, but apparently she knew this was a matter of mental toughness until Greg changed or God gave me new directions.

My best friend Linda hung in there with me as well. Even though she would hurt for me, she refrained from giving her personal opinion. I did not have to tell her much. She knew of the things Greg did and sometimes even witnessed him doing them. If I did not talk about Greg, she did not talk about Greg.

I believe everyone needs someone they can talk to during challenging times. It is important to not talk to everybody about it, for not everyone's ears are anointed to hear what you are going through. I believe it is important to wait until God brings someone that will not be a character-assassin, but will redirect conversations back to the need to stay focused on God and on staying in step with His leading.

I now love to minister about trusting God. It is different from having faith. Jesus told Peter that he was praying that Peter's faith would not fail. This statement shows that it is possible for our faith to fail. Trust, on the other hand, means that even though I have confessed what I want to see, I am trusting that God will work the situation out for my good. "And we know that all things work together for good to them that love God, to them who are the called according to his purpose" (Rom. 8:28). The Amplified Version expounds on this by saying that God is a partner in our labor. When I trust that because God is for me and no one can be against me, I can firmly believe that God will contend with those who contend with me.

For me, trusting God and depending on Him meant that I would do so even if Greg left me. The scripture that Audrey so often quoted me (Mark 10:29-30) helped prepare me for this possibility. Realizing that there was no way I could lose anything helped prepare me for the possibility of Greg leaving and gave me much added peace. Now, not only was my happiness not contingent upon Greg's behavior, but it also was not reliant upon whether he stayed with me or not. True happiness could only be found in resting in God's unwavering and unfathomable love for me.

That ye, being rooted and grounded in love, May be able to comprehend with all saints what is the breadth, and length, and depth, and height; And to know the love of Christ, which passeth knowledge, that ye might be filled with all the fullness of God.

—Ephesians 3:17-19

Laying Hold on His Plans for Me

For me to determine to trust God in this way, was somewhat like Paul's resolution to purpose to move forward in fulfilling God's plan for Him in spite of the many obstacles he was facing along the way. Making the decision was one thing, but making a plan for doing so is the step that is required. My plan included action even before action seemed to be urgently required.

First off, I would practice rejoicing no matter what. I would go beyond just being generally happy and content, and would begin to rejoice over who God is and all that He has done for me. "Finally, my brethren, rejoice in the Lord" (Phil. 3:1).

Next, I would stop acting like I was the only person going through marital challenges. "The thing that hath been, it is that which shall be; and that which is done is that which shall be done: and there is no new thing under the sun" (Eccl. 1:9). I needed to stop acting like something unique had happened to me. "There hath no temptation taken you but such as is common to man: but God is faithful, who will not suffer you to be tempted above that ye are able; but will with the temptation also make a way to escape, that ye may be able to bear it" (1 Cor.10:13).

After coming to terms with these truths, I became an intercessor for people's marriages. I would go to church and pray heartfelt prayers for marriages, other than my own, that were in trouble. I did not want anyone going through what was happening with me.

God also ministered to me one day that my marriage was a fringe benefit. The Great Commission is to be a witness for Jesus and to spread the gospel, thereby drawing others into the Kingdom of God. I could do that without being married. The call to take my focus off of myself and put it on the plan of God was broadening even wider still.

Like Paul, I needed to suffer the loss of all things in order to win Christ. This was true even though the actual loss had not occurred. At this juncture, however, it meant that I would have to view the potential of that loss as being an opportunity to continue moving forward in my relationship with Christ, even if I lost the fringe benefit of my marriage. "Yea doubtless, and I count all things but loss for the excellency of the knowledge of Christ Jesus my Lord: for whom I have suffered the loss of all things, and do count them but dung, that I may win Christ" (Phil. 3:8).

The next part of my plan was to be progressive in my quest to be more like Jesus, who had said, "My meat is to do the will of him that sent me, and to finish his work" (Jn. 4:34). I got to the point where I wanted to spend more and more time with God. At times, I wanted to be with God so much that I would give Greg money when he said he wanted to go out but did not have any money. I was having a ball at home reading God's Word and books I had purchased at the Christian bookstore.

My plan also included being progressive in my quest to know Jesus and the power of His resurrection. I could not sit back on the laurels of what God had taught me in the past, or in past accomplishments in obeying what He had shown me to do. I was to press forward, to press on through this next challenge and through others that were to come.

> *But I follow after, if that I may apprehend that for which also I am apprehended of Christ Jesus. Brethren, I count not myself to have apprehended: but this one thing I do, forgetting those things which are behind, and reaching forth unto those things which are before, I press toward the mark for the prize of the high calling of God in Christ Jesus.*
>
> —Philippians 3:12-14

Regardless of what Greg chose to do, Jesus died on the cross and was giving me gifts of life each and everyday. He had given me the strength to endure life with Greg, and He would give me the ability to continue to walk with Him even if Greg chose to leave. God's saving and His keeping power was not based on whether Greg's clothes hung in my closet.

God had a plan for my life, and my marriage to Greg might or might not be a fringe benefit. A future that included a happy marriage with Greg might or might not materialize. I would press toward the goal regardless of my circumstances.

There were days when I told God that I would help Him out if it was His will for Greg and me to no longer be together. But, God never told me to leave. You see, He had been working on Greg all along. I had no idea that the day was approaching when Greg would finally receive Jesus Christ as His Lord and Savior.

Part III: A Three-Fold Cord

Chapter Eight:
The Ultimatum

I had been offered a transfer to Atlanta, because our company was going through a period of re-organization. I could not seem to make up my mind whether to accept a layoff or be transferred to another city. I tried to include Greg in this major decision for our family. I asked him, "Greg, what do you think I should do?" He responded, "I really don't care what you do." With that, I was steaming. I could not get dressed fast enough to get to my office and accept the transfer to Atlanta.

After all the paperwork was finalized, I gave Greg the choice to come with me or stay in Mobile. All of my extended family was in Atlanta, and I felt like I would have their support there. This was not an act of financial desperation. In fact, I could have continued living in Alabama because my other choice was to accept a layoff for two years and receive 75-percent of my salary. I had been weighing my options long enough and after receiving this latest blow of Greg's cavalier attitude, I was ready to go. I wanted to get away from him.

I would move within a month, but not without Greg being true to form in every way. One would have thought there was nothing new under the sun when it came to life with Greg, but even I was surprised at the unfolding of events before I left.

For starters, I sold some of the stock I had accumulated at the company where I had been working. This would be the $3,000 I needed for the move. Greg had decided to stay in Mobile and told me he would join me later. Thanks to another one of Greg's spending sprees, I only had $125 on the day we were to move. This forced me into a position of needing to rely on Greg to help me move the furniture. I did not think I could take much more, but there was more to come. He had told me, "Oh, my good friend Kenny is going to help us."

I waited all day for him to come with good ole Kenny's truck. He was supposed to bring it to the house early so I could have all day to pack and then leave at the end of the day. He did not arrive until 1 A.M. the following morning. When he finally arrived, I asked him, "So where is the truck?"

I could not believe what was now before my eyes. All he had brought me was a pickup truck that had a big ball in the back where old cars could be hooked up and hauled away. All of my furniture and household goods were supposed to fit in the back of a pickup truck? At this point, I knew I needed to just get away!

Finally, I told him just what he wanted to hear, "You know what, keep the furniture. You can have it all. Just let me get to Atlanta. Just let me get out of here." Greg was so intoxicated that he does not remember this conversation. I told him I wanted a divorce. I had never let that come out of my mouth before. We had made an agreement early on that if we ever left each other, it would be forever. We made a decision that there would never be any breaking up and getting back together. We had agreed that "if you leave, don't come back."

We were in the bedroom when I told him that I wanted a divorce. He locked the door, stood in front of it, and told me that I didn't know what I was saying. He said he wasn't going to let me out of that room until I changed my mind. He said I was just upset and did not know what I was saying. We both sat on the bed, and he tried to console me. After about two minutes, I figured he was not going to let me out of the room until I told him that I didn't want a divorce…and so that is what I said!

I told him, "This is what we're going to agree to do: You go back and do whatever you think you want to do. Do everything you've dreamed of doing. I will never ask you what you did, and I will never allow anyone to tell me what you did, but if you should come to Georgia, then all that should be left behind." Of course, he was drunk when he said, "Yeah, Deborah, ok, that's good…that's good."

We did pack some things up and loaded them into the back of that pickup. On the drive from Alabama to Georgia, I watched my furniture fall off the truck; first one chair and then another chair. All I could think was, "I don't care, I'm leaving. I'm just leaving."

After he went back to Alabama, to have his fill of rowdy living, I told Greg, "If you make a decision to come today, I do love you, and I want you in my life. I can't say that is the way it will be tomorrow, but you'll have to take that chance."

Two months later, he joined me and the kids in Georgia. When he did, I told God, "I do not want to be out of your will, but seven years has been a long time. Do let me know if I'm wrong in saying this, but as far as I'm concerned right now he has two weeks to get this straight. I do not see why I would move to a different place, start going to a different church, and begin a new job only to have to repeat what I've been going through with him all these years. This is a new beginning for me, and I do believe that my time for living like that is over."

I went on, "Lord, I'm giving him two weeks, just two weeks. I don't want to be disobedient, but two weeks is all I can stand. I have to see some positive, real change within two weeks because I'm not going through this anymore." Greg was given a two-week period to change. I was prepared to go on with, or without, Greg Powe.

Greg's transition to Atlanta did not start off very well. His drive to Atlanta was interrupted when he was arrested for "public drunkenness" in Newnan, Georgia. He called me on the phone at about 11 p.m. and asked me to come to Newnan and pay a fine for him. Apparently, he had been drinking and had decided he was too drunk to drive any farther. After he had pulled over to the side of the road, a police officer had come along and arrested him.

This would be the last time I would help Greg because he was drunk. I called my father and asked him to ride along with me. I stopped by the ATM machine, got the needed money, and bailed him out. Up until this time, my father had no idea that things were so bad with Greg and me. He encouraged me and told me that I was home now and did not have to take this from Greg. In turn, he also encouraged Greg to do better.

Chapter Nine:
The Choice

I really was working on myself, which, in turn, was working on my marriage and affecting Greg in ways that I did not realize. The day finally came, four years after I had become a Christian, and seven years after we were married. Greg Powe received Jesus Christ as His Lord and Savior. When this happened, we were living in Atlanta.

All this time, I never had any guarantee that Greg would ever receive salvation through Jesus Christ. God never promised me that Greg would be saved. That is a choice. Everyone is a free moral agent, so it would be Greg's choice. My part was to do what I knew God wanted me to do day by day.

God had supplied me with the wisdom and the strength to stay. I cannot tell you that something great and powerful happened. As Greg would tell it, he just came to the end of himself and at long last, surrendered to God. He just came to a point in his life where he felt as though everything was falling apart.

Sin had come to a head for Greg one night after he had joined us in Atlanta and was sitting in a car in front of a nightclub. He was with a strange woman he did not know when God started speaking to him in a way that made him take stock of where he was in life. Here he was in Atlanta with no job, getting ready to go drinking with a woman he did not know. Suddenly, he realized that his life was anything but successful. As he came to the conclusion, Satan told him, "I will give you back what you had." God simply said, "I've been here for you all along." With that, he asked the lady to get out of the car and he came home.

It would be years before I learned of that experience. My first clue that change was on the horizon was when I found out he had been going to Bible studies and not telling me.

I got quite a surprise from him one day when I came home from work. It was raining, and he ran out to the car and said, "You're late, you're late." Puzzled, I asked, "What do you mean, you're late?" He said, "I'm late for Bible study." Of course, I was skeptical. "Sure," I thought as I handed him the car key and he left.

Much to my surprise, it was not a scam. He really was going to a Bible study. He had been going, but had not told me about it. In fact, that was just the start of many more Bible studies to come. He kept going to one Bible study after another, night after night.

Before long, he was going to five Bible studies a week. He was just eating the Word of God. Sometimes, I would wake up because I had just rolled over Bibles and books he had been studying in bed before he had fallen asleep.

Apparently, it had all started with changes in me. My decision to do what God told me to do caused my husband to see and want what I had in God. When I asked him later what had happened, he said, "I just kept watching you, and your life seemed good. It looked to me like I was trying my best to make life bad for you, but everything kept working out well for you. God kept blessing you in spite of all that I was doing to you."

For example, Greg had seen that even though he was not working and was not contributing financially to the household, all of mine and the children's needs were being provided for. When I needed a car, God blessed me with a car. Another example was that I was increasing financially on my job while he drifted from one job to the next.

My decision to obey God had brought blessings to me that surprised even Greg. The goodness of God had been provoking Greg to jealousy similar to how God provoked the Jews to jealousy when they saw how He was blessing the Gentiles (see Romans 11:11).

Greg had seen my happiness and the wisdom God gave me through all of my hardships. He had seen the fruit of me saying to God at the start of each morning, "It's me and You God." I had been having wonderful days with God while Greg was having horrible days with the devil.

Greg had not understood what was going on in my life, but he did see the fruit of my faith. I had become pretty unshakeable in my peace no matter what turmoil Greg had thrown at me.

All the while God had me working on myself, He had been working on behalf of my marriage. He had been using me to work on Greg, but in a very different way than I would have worked on him myself. Nothing Greg was doing surprised God. He knew exactly how to bring him to the breaking point. I would have tried to hound Greg into straightening up. God, on the other hand, had provoked him to jealousy by allowing him to spiral to the point where he was at the end of himself.

While God was at work in me, He had been lifting me up as an example to Greg. Sure, Greg went through a range of emotions that made the situation look even more hopeless than ever. But through it all, God was drawing Greg to Himself. And by drawing Greg to Himself, He was actually working to fulfill the desire of my heart to have a husband I could trust and a marriage that would bring me and my children peace and happiness.

Much to my surprise, in an indirect way, the Word of God was dividing soul and spirit. God was using His Word to transform both of us, me directly and Greg indirectly.

> *For the word of God is quick, and powerful, and sharper than any two- edged sword, piercing even to the dividing asunder of soul and spirit, and of the joints and marrow, and is a discerner of the thoughts and intents of the heart.*
>
> —Hebrews 4:12

Until that point, I was judging only by what I could see. I had given him a two-week ultimatum because it appeared that nothing had changed. This also is why I was completely shocked when he started digging into the Word of God with gusto and never turned back.

Although God did use my testimony, or my conversation, to provoke Greg to take that eternal step to receive Jesus as the Lord of his life, Greg made the choice to serve God rather than Satan. He was the one who chose to reject Satan's offer to put him "back on top again." He was the one who decided to receive the love of the One who had "been there for him all along."

Now, I'm so grateful to God that I obeyed him and stayed with Greg. I now tell Christians who have an unsaved spouse or loved one: If he/she is still living and breathing, there is still a chance.

God can fix whatever is broken because He is a miracle-working God. I want to emphasize here that, in some instances, people will not allow the power of God to prevail. It will only work if both partners agree to continue on in the marriage. Because only God knows the heart and intentions of man; the Holy Spirit must be the One to guide a person in what decision to make about this. When God directs a particular course of action, He will also give the wisdom and strength to see it through if the person continues to focus on Him. It is important to not be paralyzed too long with indecisiveness. Once the decision is made, God can bring a person back on course, if the decision made is not in line with His will. If the decision is right, He will give you all the wisdom and strength to endure. Once I had made my decision, God was able to get on with shaping my character. This would not have been possible if I was confused about whether I would stay with Greg.

Chapter Ten:
Unexpected Challenges

Even though I had been praying for four years for my husband to become a Christian, it was hard for me to keep pace with how quickly the changes came after he was born-again. He immediately began studying the Word and applying it to his life as quickly as humanly possible. He became an extremist. If God said it, he was going to do it even if he did not understand it.

One day he came home and announced, "God says I am the head of the house. Deborah, you've been taking care of the bills and handling bill collectors all these years, and that is just wrong. I need to take my role. Give me the checkbook."

My mind immediately went into overdrive: He had not done well with money. He didn't even know how much money I made. I was deeply concerned that he would take all the money we had and spend it on something crazy. My mind was saying, "You are going to make our credit worse. It is going to be bad. I do not want to do this," but the Word of God was saying, "Submit." I pleaded with God, "How can I submit to this? Greg doesn't know what he's doing."

I knew my husband's approach to banking well. He always thought his balance was equal to the figure the bank teller gave him when he called the bank. He never took outstanding checks into account. Time and again, we would bounce one check after another whenever he had been in charge of the banking.

I did submit to his request to take charge of paying the bills and managing our bank account. I was in prayer during much of this period of time. I did not want overdraft charges to skyrocket so high that we would end up in another hole. Our credit was already shot, but we were working on establishing a good pay-history. Greg even contacted the Internal Revenue Service and filed seven years of tax returns. Greg really wanted to be a man of integrity. When I brought this situation before the Lord, I would pray, "God, my husband is really trying to do what he believes you want him to do. Please help me—please help us—concerning this."

At times, I would ask God to please make it possible for this or that check not to bounce, and many times, He was faithful even in that. It is not possible for a person to "float" a check in that way anymore, because checks clear immediately now.

Eventually, Greg gave me back the responsibility for managing our funds and dealing with our creditors, but not before I had first submitted this area of our lives to God and to Greg.

As Greg grew in the Lord, so did I. I grew as a person, and I grew as a wife. I was so thankful that God had given me the wonderful fringe benefit of having a good marriage. In Greg, God gave me much more than I could have ever dreamed to ask of Him. He gave me a husband who is now the pastor of a church and a wonderful father to our four children, two of whom are now grown and living on their own.

Periodically, I will simply ask the question, "Greg, is there something that I can do to make things better? Is there some area you would like me to change in?" Of course, I also tell him not to give me a huge list. I say, "Let's just start with one thing at a time."

I ask him this because I have learned that love does not develop by osmosis. Just because I love Greg does not mean that I know what he is thinking. I have to spend time with him to know what he has on his heart and to look for ways for us to help our love grow. I also ask him this because I know that being the wife God has called me to be is an ever changing and ever evolving process. I do not want to leave any room in my marriage for frustration, so I have taken the guesswork out of it.

I also know that words are powerful. This is why I often refer to myself as the "good wife." When I do something he likes, I say, "Yeah, that is what the good wife does. I'm the good wife." Now, he also often calls me "the good wife."

This has paved the way for me to playfully ask him, "Well then, what is it that the 'good wife' can do to improve?" My playfulness brings us a good laugh, but it also strengthens "our good marriage" that is a wonderful fringe benefit of serving a "a very good God."

Oh, yes…His response:

"Don't ever change. I love you forever."

And the greatest thing about that is I know he means it!

Chapter Eleven
Where Are We Now?

These past twenty years have been excellent. It has been a time of growing and increasing in the Lord. Oh, we have had challenges, but now we face everything together.

We are sure our move to Atlanta was ordered by God. That is where Greg was born again and where we met our pastors, Dr. Creflo A. Dollar and Pastor Taffi Dollar. Dr. Dollar played a crucial part in developing the man that my husband is today, and he and Pastor Taffi are still a vital part of our lives. Dr. Creflo A. Dollar and Pastor Taffi Dollar mean more to Greg and me than words can express. He taught my husband how to be a father, a husband and a man of integrity. We will always be grateful to God for their obedience to the Word and their dedication to change lives.

During our time in Atlanta, two more beautiful children were born to us. I recall Greg asking me about having more children now that we were both born-again. My answer was a solid "yes." On January 13, 1986, Bryan Michael was born. Fifteen months later, on April 22, 1987, God granted the desire of Greg's heart for us to have a girl, and Chrystle Nicole was born.

Our three sons have graduated from high school. Gregory is working for the ministry and attending college as he prepares for a higher position in ministry. Christopher has completed college and is the director of our Graphics Department. Bryan is in college preparing for a position in ministry while running a sound production company he formed. Chrystle, having recently graduated from high school, will also be attending college to prepare for a position in ministry. They all love the Lord and are very active in our church.

We now are pastors of a church in Tampa, Florida, that has an average weekly attendance of 5,000 people. We have a television ministry and we travel throughout the Caribbean and parts of Europe as our mission field. We recently opened a second church located in St. Petersburg, Florida.

We also have an assignment from God to build three convention centers: one in Tampa, Florida, one in the Dallas/Ft. Worth, Texas area and one on the West Coast. These convention centers will be for the use of the Body of Christ to minister to the masses that are being added to the Kingdom of God. Public facilities are not as accessible to the Body of Christ as they once were and the cost to rent them is outrageous. Because these facilities will belong to the Body of Christ, regardless of denomination, anyone preaching the Word of God will have access to these facilities.

We are well on our way, having acquired 204 acres of land in Tampa, in addition to the facility where we now hold services. With the support of "Truth Partners" all around the world, we are moving forward with this project debt-free.

Is it not just like God to give such a vision to a man like Greg Powe, one who lived on the edge when he was unsaved and is just as extreme for God now that he is saved?

> *I am indeed enjoying life in overflowing fullness. The thief comes only in order to steal and kill and destroy. I came that they may have and enjoy life, and have it in abundance (to the full, till it overflows).* —*John 10:10 AMP*

Chapter Twelve:
So, Where Are You Now?

The hardest thing to do, most of the time, is release your spouse totally to God. For whatever reason, we seem to want to help God out. We do have a part, but normally it is not so vocal. Most of the time, it is our lifestyle that will cause them to desire God. Once your spouse commits himself to the Lord, victory is assured.

You see, God has a purpose for everyone's life and until a man knows that purpose, he wanders around aimlessly searching for something to fill that void.

We have to see our husband as God does - someone who has not yet found their way. Jesus said, He is the Way, the Truth and the Life and He has said come unto Me you who are heavy laden and burdened down and I will give you rest. That is the place we want our spouses to be, setting at the feet of Jesus, seeking His face and carrying out the will of the Lord. When that takes place, he will then know how to love you as Christ loves the church and gave His life for it.

For you who are in a similar situation as I was in, you have to know that God is available to help you. But there are some things you must put in order.

1. Make a decision to stay or not. Neither God nor anyone else can counsel indecision. You must pray and ask God if this is a situation you should stay in. Don't be hesitant. If you make the wrong choice, God will correct you. If you make the right

choice, God will give you all the wisdom you need to handle the decision (see James 1:5-7).

2. Trust God. You must know that God wants the best for you and you must trust Him with your present and your future (see Proverbs 3:5).

3. You must come to a place of peace even in your turmoil, understanding that peace is not the absence of trouble, but the presence of God in the trouble (see Phil. 4:6-7).

4. Let the peace of God rule and allow peace to lead you. Once a decision is made, you must be ready for the attack against that decision. You must always go back to the point where you found peace and let that decision stand (see Isaiah 55:12 and Col.3:15).

5. Seek wisdom from God. He will give it to you for your particular situation. He actually has stored up wisdom for the righteous (see Proverbs 3:7 and James 1:5).

6. Relinquish your husband to God totally. Don't be afraid (see Mark 10:29-30).

7. Find a true friend who will be an encouragement and a sounding board for difficult times (see Proverbs 17:17).

8. Do not murmur and complain, but do everything as unto the Lord (see Phil. 2:4).

9. Pray the will of God for your husband. Do not pray selfishly (see 1 John 5:14-15).

10. You are accountable for upholding the scriptures as it pertains to you as a wife (see Ephesians 5:33, AMP).

Finally, I tell you to work on your own relationship with God. It is the only one you are responsible for. He will build you up and make you strong.

Let your character or moral disposition be free from love of money (including greed, avarice, lust, and craving for earthly possessions) and be satisfied with your present circumstances and with what you have); for He God Himself has said, I will not in any way, fail you nor give you up nor leave you without support. (I will not, I will not, I will not) in any degree leave you helpless nor forsake nor let you down relax My hold you, (Assuredly not!)."

—Hebrews 13:5 AMP

"I have told you these things, so that in Me you may have (perfect) peace and confidence. In the world you have tribulation and trials and distress and frustration: but be of good cheer (take courage be confident, certain undaunted)! For I

have overcome the world. (I have deprived it of power to harm you and have conquered it for you.)

—John 16:33 AMP

"...I came that they may have and enjoy life, and have it in abundance to the full, till it overflows."

—John 10:10 AMP

My prayer is that the peace of God shall mount guard and garrison over your hearts and minds in Christ Jesus (see Phil. 4:7, AMP).

Deborah H. Powe, 1972

Pastor Greg and Deborah Powe in front of Kathleen Mitchell Elementary School, First Meeting Place of WCCI.

Marriage Vow Renewal, 9 Years

Pastor Greg and Deborah Powe, 1989

Flora Hunter (far left-Greg's Mother), Emma Stodghill (Far right-Deborah's Mother) Pastor Greg and Deborah Powe at his first Pastor Appreciation 1993

Pastor Greg Powe and Deborah, 2003

Pastor Greg and Deborah Powe in their new home, 200

Gregory Alexander 5 Months

Gregory Alexander 22 Years

Christopher 7 Months

Christopher 18 Years

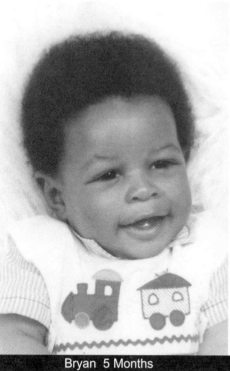

Bryan 5 Months

Bryan 18 Years

Chrystle 6 months

Chrystle 18 Years

Pastor Powe and His Family, 2003
Christopher, Bryan, Pastor Powe, Deborah, Gregory and Chrystle

Pastor Greg Powe's 50th Birthday Celebration

Marriage Vow Renewal, 2005